PIANO • VOCAL • CHORDS

Love That Movie Music

Alfred

ISBN 0-7579-4082-X (Book)

CONTENTS

ACROSS THE STARS
(LOVE THEME FROM *STAR WARS*®: EPISODE II)

Music by
JOHN WILLIAMS

Moderately slow and gently (♩ = 76)

(with pedal)

Across the Stars - 5 - 1

4

Appassionato

From THE MOTORCYCLE DIARIES

AL OTRO LADO DEL RÍO

Letra y Música por
JORGE ABNER DREXLER

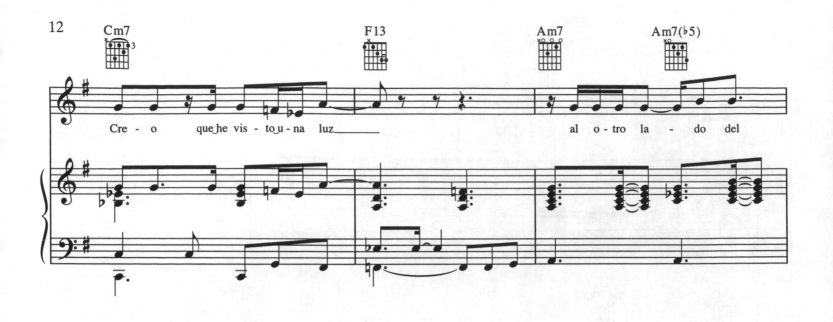

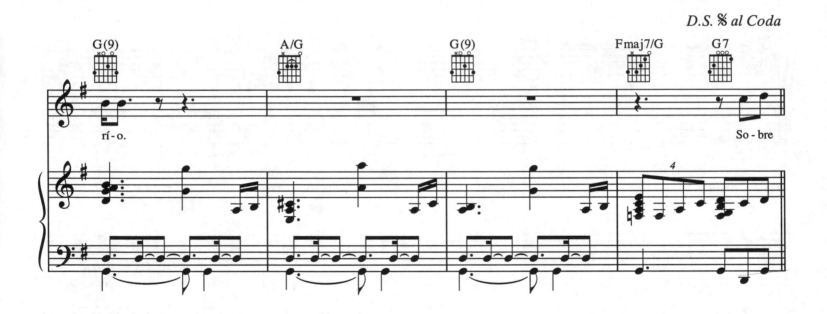

From the LUCASFILM LTD. Production "STAR WARS: Episode I The Phantom Menace"

ANAKIN'S THEME

By
JOHN WILLIAMS

Anakin's Theme - 3 - 1

AMERICA'S AVIATION HERO
(from THE AVIATOR)

Composed by
HOWARD SHORE

Moderately (♩ = 88)

(with pedal)

America's Aviation Hero - 2 - 1

appassionata

ANOTHER DUMB BLONDE

Words and Music by
TIM JAMES and ANTONINA ARMATO

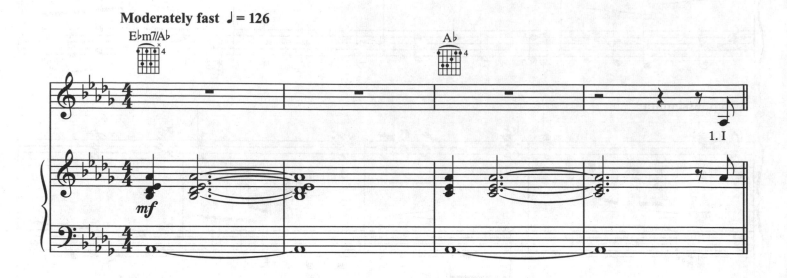

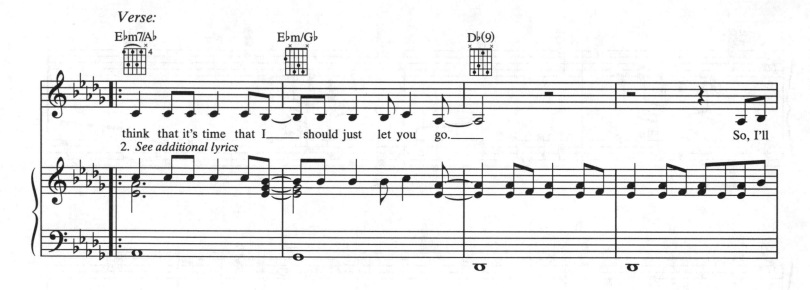

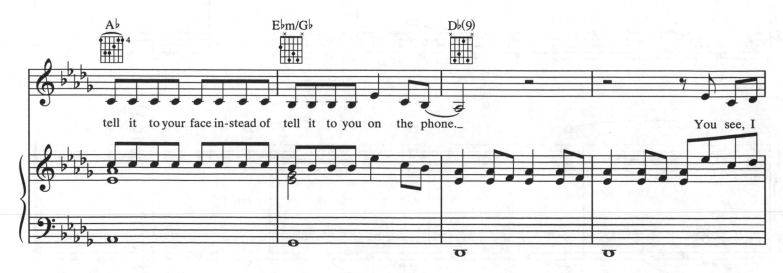

Another Dumb Blonde - 5 - 1

Bridge:

Oh, no. ___ ___ not me, ___ no no.

You want just a lit-tle tro-phy hang-in' on your wall so all your friends will

see you got it go-in' on. But I see what you are, so clear-ly. But, ba-by,

ba-by, baby, that's not al-right with me.___ That's al-right, that's o-kay, I

22

Verse 2:
Last night I went to a party, hoping I'd see you there.
And sure enough, you were hanging on some other girl, playing with her hair.
And I overheard you telling her the very same thing you said to me the night before.
Hook, line and sinker, you were walking with her out the door.
(To Chorus:)

BATTLE OF THE HEROES

(From *Star Wars*®: Episode III *Revenge of the Sith*)

Music by
JOHN WILLIAMS

Battle of the Heroes - 7 - 1

24

From the Motion Picture AUSTIN POWERS: The Spy Who Shagged Me

BEAUTIFUL STRANGER

Words and Music by
MADONNA CICCONE and WILLIAM ORBIT

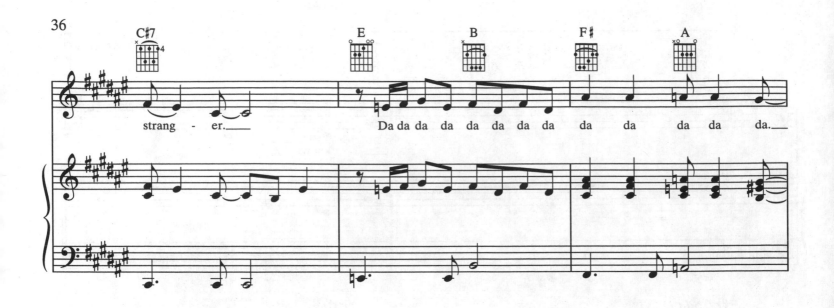

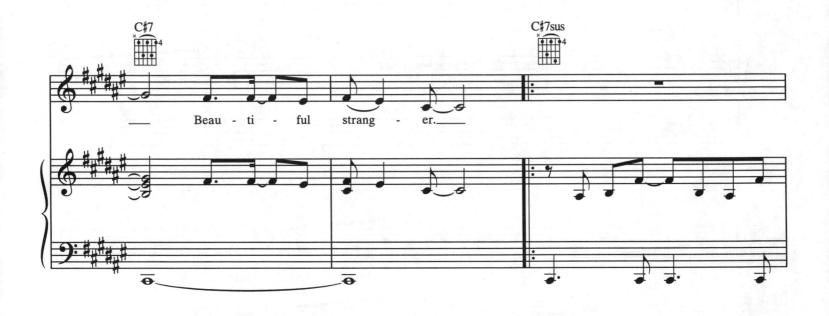

BECAUSE YOU LOVED ME
(Theme from "Up Close & Personal")

Words and Music by
DIANE WARREN

Slowly ♩ = 76

Verse:

1. For all those times you stood by me, for all the
   wings and made me fly, you touched my

truth that you made me see, for all the joy you brought to my life, for all the
hand, I could touch the sky. I lost my faith you gave it back to me. You said no

wrong that you made right, for ev-ery dream you made come true, for all the
star was out of reach, you stood by me and I stood tall. I had your

Because You Loved Me - 5 - 1

From THE POLAR EXPRESS

BELIEVE

Words and Music by
GLEN BALLARD and ALAN SILVESTRI

Moderately slow ♩ = 80

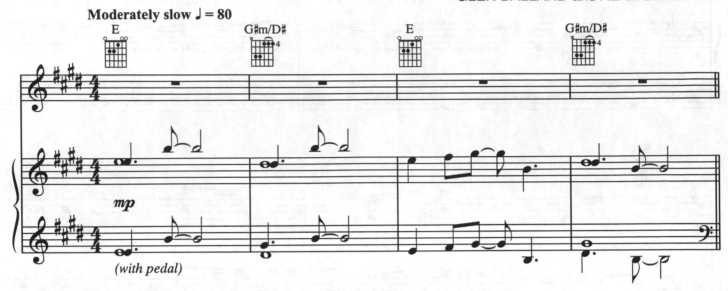

(with pedal)

Verse:

1. Chil - dren___ sleep - ing,___ snow is soft - ly fall - ing.___
2. Trains move___ quick - ly___ to their jour - ney's end.

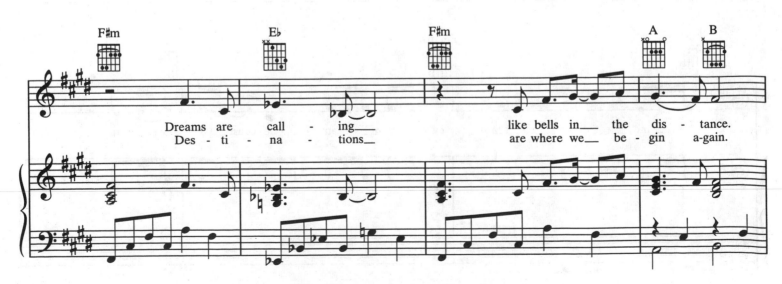

Dreams are call - ing___ like bells in___ the dis - tance.
Des - ti - na - tions___ are where we___ be - gin a - gain.

44

BELIEVER

Words and Music by
will.i.am and John Legend

Slowly and freely ♩ = 84

Verse:

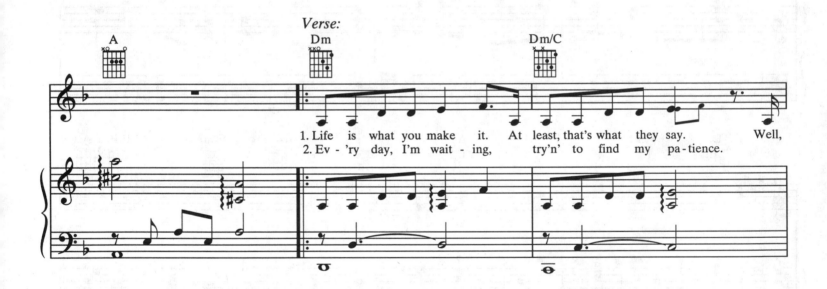

1. Life is what you make it. At least, that's what they say. Well,
2. Ev - 'ry day, I'm wait - ing, try'n' to find my pa - tience.

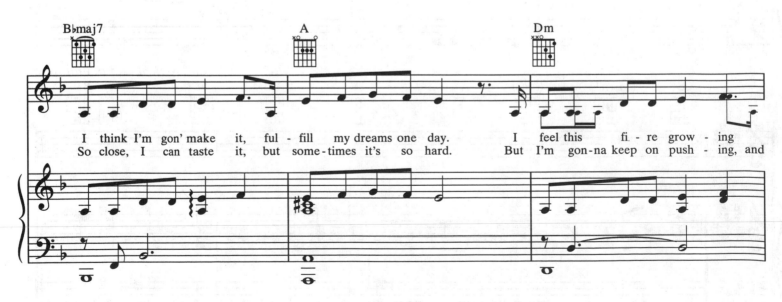

I think I'm gon' make it, ful - fill my dreams one day. I feel this fi - re grow - ing
So close, I can taste it, but some - times it's so hard. But I'm gon - na keep on push - ing, and

Believer - 4 - 1

deep in - side of me. I'm so in - spir - ed know - ing that it's my des - ti - ny. }
I'm gon-na keep on fight - ing, and I'm gon-na keep on try - ing, be - cause I've come too far. } I

Pre-chorus:

breathe like a cham - pion, I dream I'm a cham - pion, I see I'm a cham - pion, it's

meant to be. My will's get - ting strong - er, I can't wait an - y long - er. I'm

Chorus:

sing - ing a song that's in - side of me.__ 'Cause I'm_____ a be -

Believer - 4 - 2

be-liev - ing. be-liev - ing.
(I__ keep be-liev-ing, I__ keep be-liev-ing, I__ keep be-

liev-ing, be-liev - ing. be-liev - ing. be-liev - ing.)
liev-ing, I__ keep be-liev-ing, I__ keep be-liev-ing, The

fu - ture is now,__ it__ starts_____ to - day._____

rit.

BLUE MORGAN
(from MILLION DOLLAR BABY)

Composed by
CLINT EASTWOOD

Freely and flowing (♩ = 60)

Blue Morgan - 2 - 1

BORN TO RIDE

Words and Music by
WILLIAM ROSS, ROXANNE SEEMAN
and GAVIN GREENAWAY

55

up, but I will nev - er give up you see,

nothing is stop - ping me.

Instrumental solo:

Born to Ride - 6 - 4

Verse 3:

3. I'll go where life leads me, through it all,

fear - less and free. Wild rose of the

des - ert, with the wind by my side, I was born

BREAKAWAY

Words and Music by
MATTHEW GERRARD, AVRIL LAVIGNE
and BRIDGET BENENATE

60

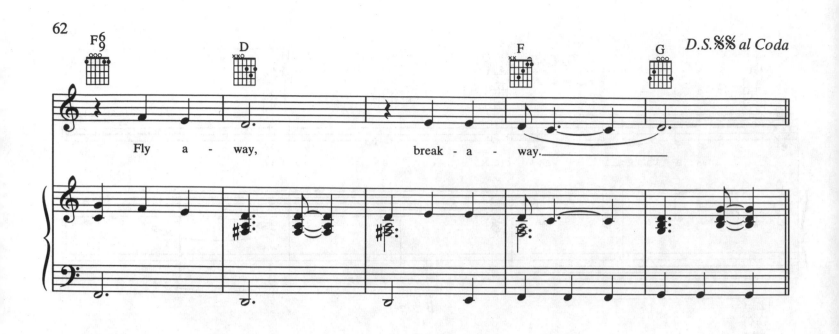

Fly a - way, break - a - way._____

⊕ Coda

break - a - way,_____ break -

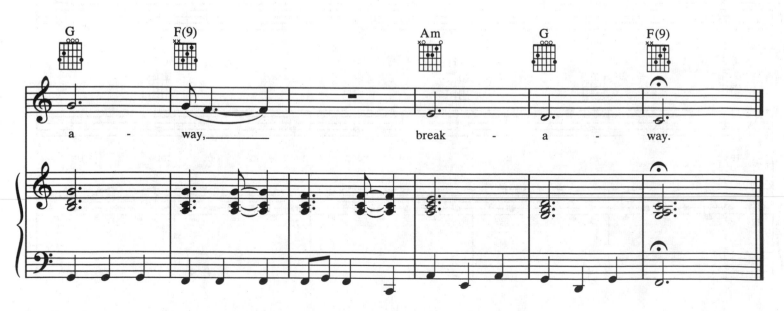

a - way,_____ break - a - way.

CAN'T FIGHT THE MOONLIGHT
(Theme from Coyote Ugly)

Words and Music by
DIANE WARREN

Can't Fight the Moonlight - 5 - 1

66

Bridge:

Chorus:

From the Warner Bros. Motion Picture THE PERFECT STORM

COMING HOME FROM THE SEA

By JAMES HORNER

Slowly (♩ = 56)

(with pedal)

Slightly faster

Coming Home From the Sea - 6 - 1

Faster (♩=116)

72

From Warner Bros. Pictures' HARRY POTTER AND THE PRISONER OF AZKABAN

DOUBLE TROUBLE

Music by
JOHN WILLIAMS

Medieval in spirit (♩ = 92)

Spiritedly

Dou - ble, dou - ble toil and trou - ble; fire____ burn and caul - dron bub - ble.

Dou - ble, dou - ble toil and trou - ble; some - thing wick - ed this way comes!

Double Trouble - 5 - 1

Driving now, with a "swagger"

78

fire_____ burn and caul - dron bub - ble.

fire_____ burn and bub - ble.___

Dou - ble, dou - ble toil and trou - ble; fire_____ burn and caul - dron bub - ble.

Dou - ble, dou - ble toil and trou - ble; fire_____ burn and caul - dron

Forcefully

bub - ble._____ Some - thing wick - ed this way comes!

f

GOLDFINGER

Lyric by LESLIE BRICUSSE
and ANTHONY NEWLEY
Music by JOHN BARRY

* Original recording in E.

Goldfinger - 3 - 1

From Warner Bros. Pictures SPACE COWBOYS

ESPACIO

Composed by
CLINT EASTWOOD

Espacio - 2 - 1

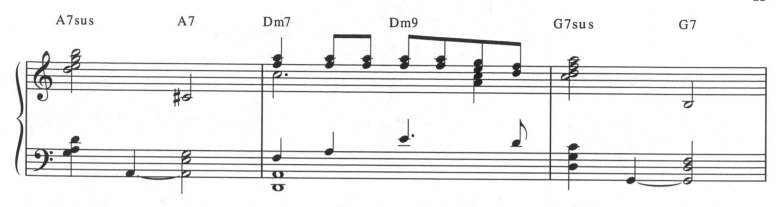

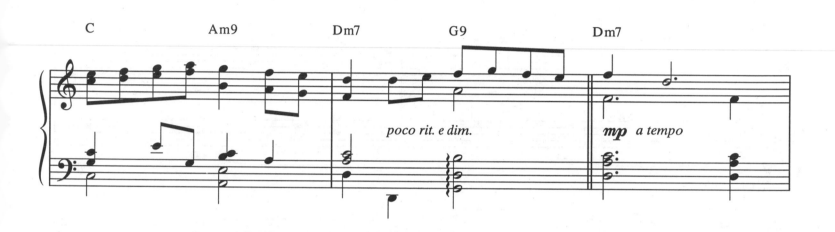

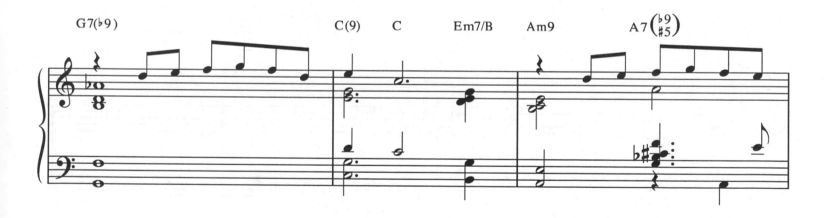

Espacio - 2 - 2

GOLLUM'S SONG

as performed by Emiliana Torrini in the motion picture
"The Lord of the Rings: The Two Towers"

Words by FRAN WALSH
Music by HOWARD SHORE

Gollum's Song - 5 - 1

From Warner Bros. Pictures' HARRY POTTER AND THE SORCERER'S STONE
HEDWIG'S THEME

Music by
JOHN WILLIAMS

Hedwig's Theme - 5 - 1

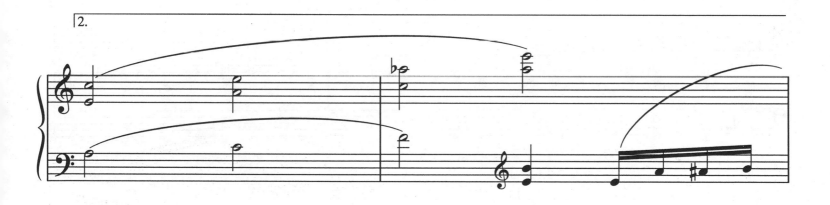

Hedwig's Theme - 5 - 5

From the Columbia Pictures Motion Picture SPIDER-MAN

HERO

Words and Music by
CHAD KROEGER

Slowly ♩. = 48

Verse 1:

1. I am so___ high,___ I can hear___ heav - en.___

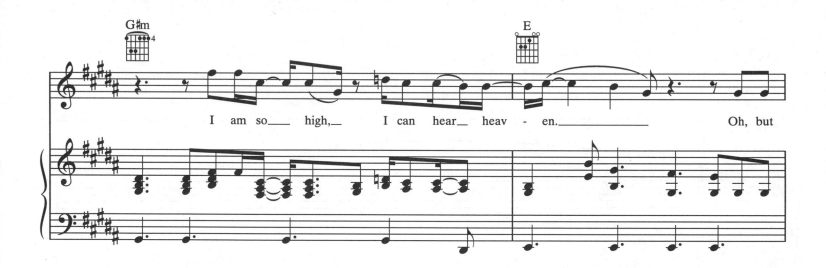

I am so___ high,___ I can hear___ heav - en.___ Oh, but

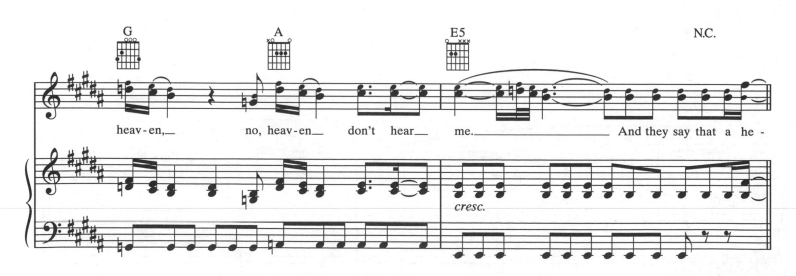

heav - en,___ no, heav-en___ don't hear___ me.___ And they say that a he-

Hero - 6 - 1

96

Hero - 6 - 3

98

Hero - 6 - 6

From the Touchstone Motion Picture "CON AIR"

HOW DO I LIVE

Words and Music by
DIANE WARREN

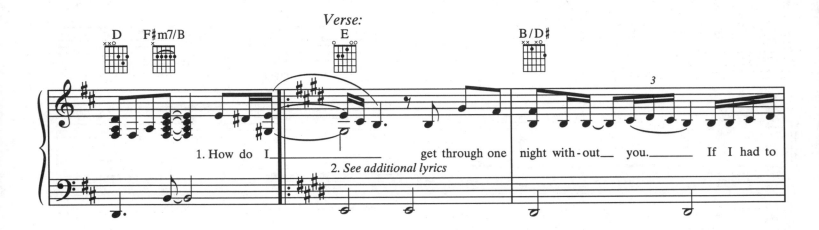

1. How do I get through one night with-out you. If I had to
2. *See additional lyrics*

live with-out you, what kind of life would that be? Oh, I, I need you in my

arms, need you to hold. You're my world, my heart, my soul. If you ev-er leave,

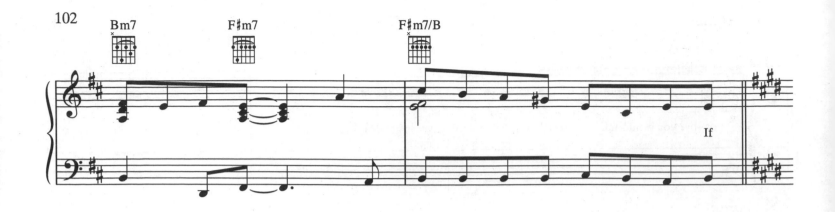

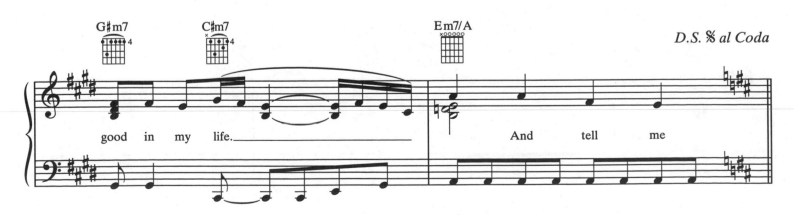

Coda

now how do I, oh, how do I live

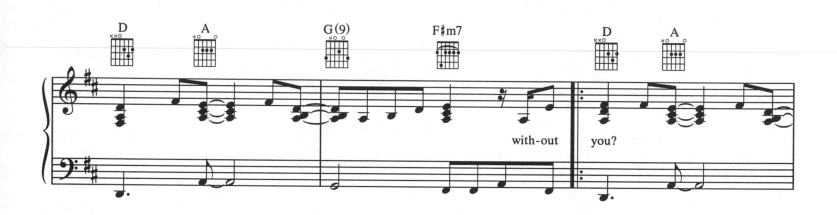

with-out you?

*Repeat ad lib. and fade
(vocal 1st time only)*

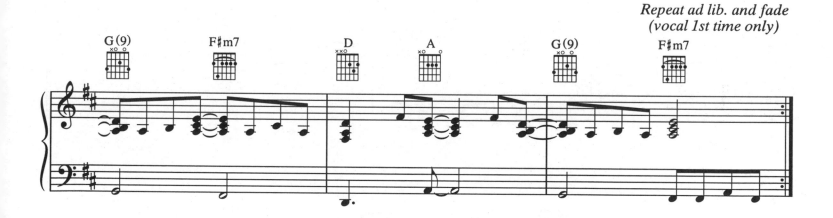

Verse 2:
Without you, there'd be no sun in my sky,
There would be no love in my life,
There'd be no world left for me.
And I, baby, I don't know what I would do,
I'd be lost if I lost you.
If you ever leave,
Baby, you would take away everything real in my life.
And tell me now...
(To Chorus:)

From Touchstone Pictures' ARMAGEDDON

I DON'T WANT TO MISS A THING

Words and Music by
DIANE WARREN

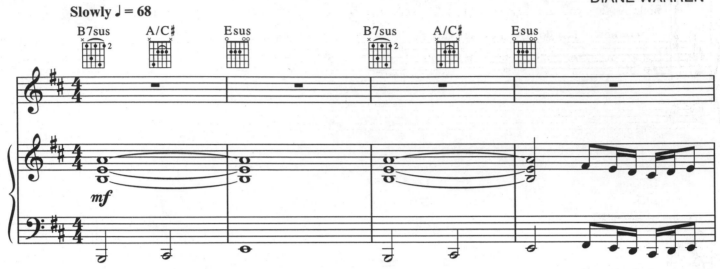

1. I could

Verse 1:

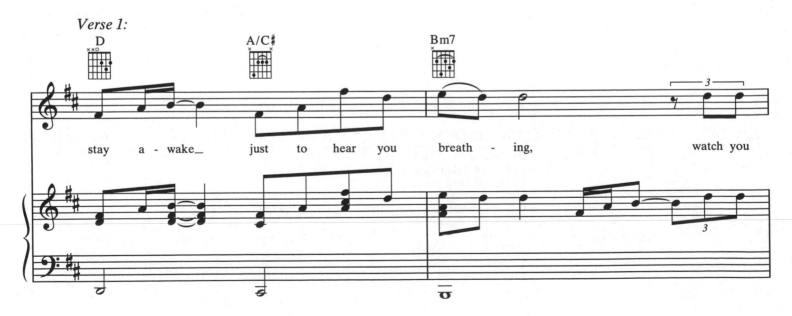

stay a - wake_ just to hear you breath - ing, watch you

I Don't Want to Miss a Thing - 7 - 1

108

Chorus:

Repeat ad lib. and fade

I'M ALIVE

Words and Music by
KRISTIAN LUNDIN and ANDREAS CARLSSON

Moderately ♩ = 104

Mmm,_____ mmm._____

I get wings to fly,

oh,_____ I'm a-live,_____ yeah.__

(Drums)

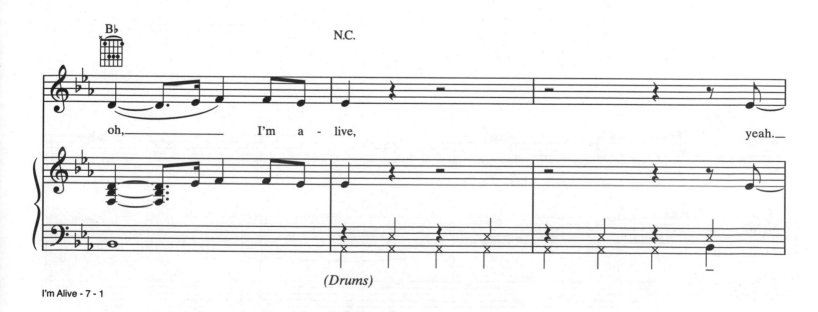

I'm Alive - 7 - 1

§ *Chorus:*

When you call on me, when I hear you breathe, I get wings to fly. I feel_____ that___ I'm a-live. When you

IN DREAMS
(featured in "The Breaking Of The Fellowship")

Words and Music by
FRAN WALSH and
HOWARD SHORE

In Dreams - 3 - 1

INTO THE WEST

Words and Music by
FRAN WALSH, HOWARD SHORE, ANNIE LENNOX

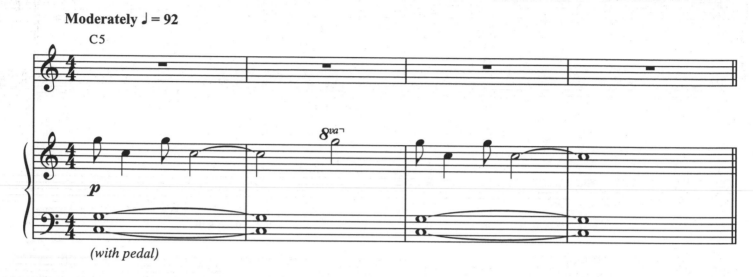

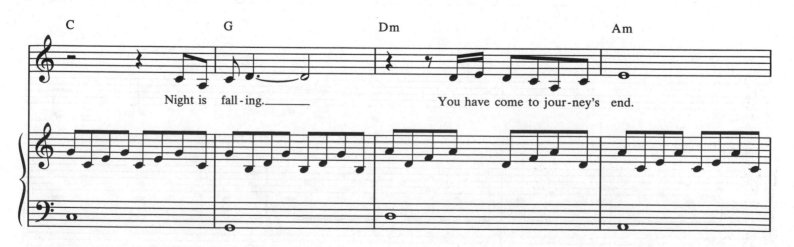

Into the West - 7 - 1

122

124

Why do the white gulls call?

A - cross the sea,

a pale moon ris - es. The ships have

come to car - ry you home.

here_____ in my arms_____ just

D.S. 𝄋 al Coda

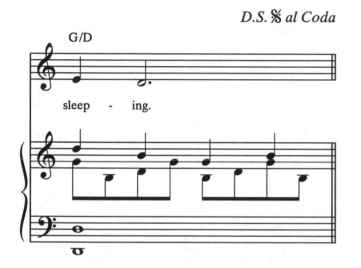

sleep - ing.

Coda

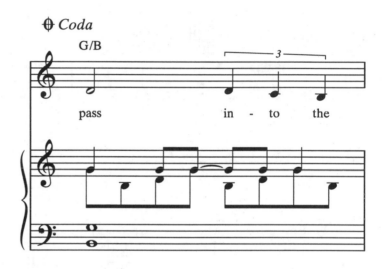

pass in - to the

West._____

rit. e dim.

JAMES BOND THEME
(Bond vs. Oakenfold)

Music by MONTY NORMAN
Remix by PAUL OAKENFOLD

James Bond Theme - 5 - 1

With a slight swing feel

To Coda ⊕

James Bond Theme - 5 - 2

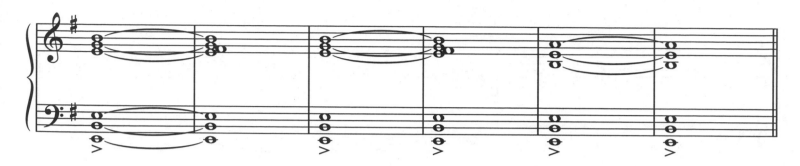

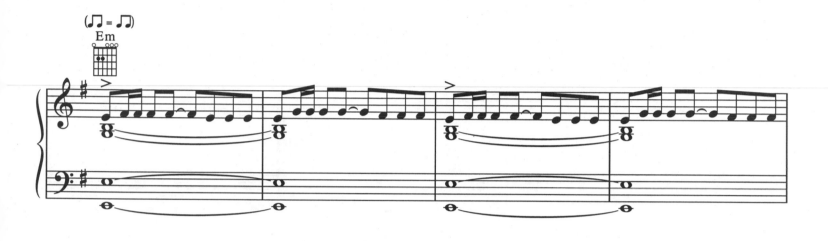

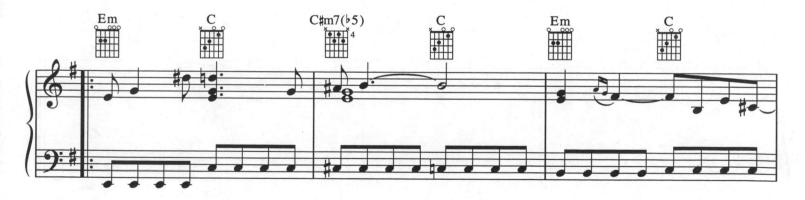

James Bond Theme - 5 - 4

LOVE STORY (THEME)

Words and Music by
CARL SIGMAN and FRANCIS LAI

Where Do I Be-gin _____ to tell the sto-ry of how great a love can be, _____
With her first hel-lo _____ she gave a mean-ing to this emp-ty world of mine; _____

— The sweet love sto-ry that is old-er than the sea, The sim-ple truth a-bout the
— There'd nev-er be an-oth-er love, an-oth-er time; She came in-to my life and

love she brings to me? _____ Where do I start? _____
made the liv-ing fine. _____

134

Love Story (Theme) - 3 - 2

From the Miramax Motion Picture "Music of the Heart"

MUSIC OF MY HEART

Words and Music by
DIANE WARREN

Music of My Heart - 6 - 1

done for my__ soul._____ You'll nev - er know__ the gift__ you've__
see - ing me__ through._____ You were the song__ that al - ways__

__ giv - en me.____ I'll car - ry it with me.___
__ made me sing.____ I'm sing - ing this for you.___

Through the days__ a - head,__ I think__ of days__ be - fore,__ when you made me
Ev - 'ry - where__ I go,__ I think__ of where_ I've been__ and of the

MYSTIC RIVER THEME

By
CLINT EASTWOOD

Mystic River Theme - 2 - 1

THE NOTEBOOK
(Main Title)

Written by
AARON ZIGMAN

Slowly, with expression (♩ = 58)

Più mosso

A little faster (♩ = 69)

The Notebook - 3 - 1

From Touchstone Pictures' PEARL HARBOR

THERE YOU'LL BE

Words and Music by
DIANE WARREN

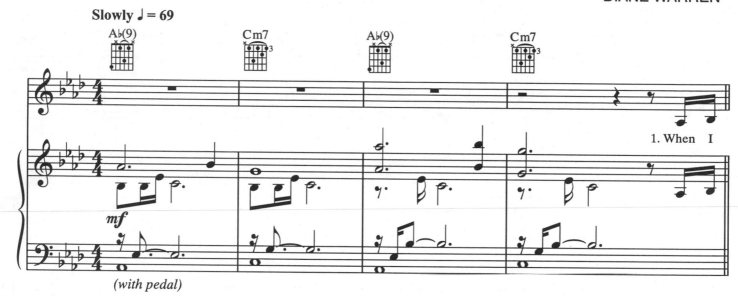

Verse:

think back on____ these times____ and the dreams we left___ be - hind,___ I'll be
showed me how___ it feels___ to feel the sky with - in___ my reach.___ And I

glad 'cuz I____ was blessed___ to get,___ to have you in my___ life.___ When I
al - ways will___ re - mem - ber all___ the strength you gave to___ me.___ Your love

There You'll Be - 5 - 1

150

OVER THE RAINBOW

Lyric by
E.Y. HARBURG

Music by
HAROLD ARLEN

Over the Rainbow - 4 - 1

THE PINK PANTHER

Music by
HENRY MANCINI

From Warner Bros. Pictures' TROY

REMEMBER

Words by
CYNTHIA WEIL

Music by
JAMES HORNER

last light_____ to fade in-to the ris - ing sun.
lis - ten,_____ you'll hear me call a-cross the sky.

I'm
As

with_____ you when-ev - er you tell_____ my sto - ry, for
long_____ as I still can reach out_____ and touch you, for then

I_____ am all I've done.
I_____ will nev - er

Re-

163

mem - ber, when your dreams have end - ed, time can be tran - scend - ed. I live for-
ah,

ev - er, re - mem - ber me. Re - mem - ber me. Re -
Ah.

mem - ber me.
Ah.

decresc.

mp   a tempo   rit.

Remember - 6 - 6

SECONDHAND LIONS
(Main Theme)

Composed by
PATRICK DOYLE

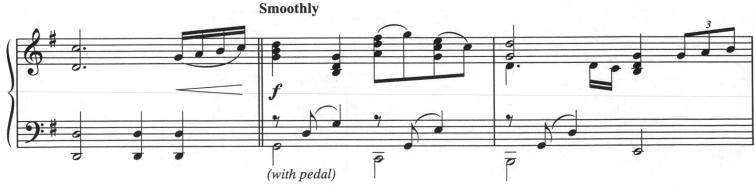

Secondhand Lions - 2 - 1

a little slower

SONG FROM "M*A*S*H"
(Suicide Is Painless)

Words and Music by
MIKE ALTMAN and JOHNNY MANDEL

Moderately (Folk - Gospel Feeling)

Through ear-ly morn-ing fog___ I see___ vis-ions of ___ the things ___ to be: ___ the pains that are ___ with-held ___ for me. ___ I re - a - lize ___ and I ___ can see, _____ that su - i - cide ___ is pain - less, it brings on man - y chang-

Song From "M*A*S*H" - 2 - 1

1. Try to find a way to make
   All our little joys relate
   Without that ever-present hate
   But now I know that it's too late.
     And, Chorus

3. The game of life is hard to play,
   I'm going to lose it anyway,
   The losing card I'll someday lay,
   So this is all I have to say,
     That: Chorus

4. The only way to win, is cheat
   And lay it down before I'm beat,
   And to another give a seat
   For that's the only painless feat.
     'Cause: Chorus

5. The sword of time will pierce our skins,
   It doesn't hurt when it begins
   But as it works it's way on in,
   The pain grows stronger, watch it grin.
     For: Chorus

6. A brave man once requested me
   To answer questions that are key,
   Is it to be or not to be
   And I replied; "Oh, why ask me."
     'Cause: Chorus

STAR WARS
(Main Title)

Music by
JOHN WILLIAMS

March (Majestic)

Star Wars - 2 - 1

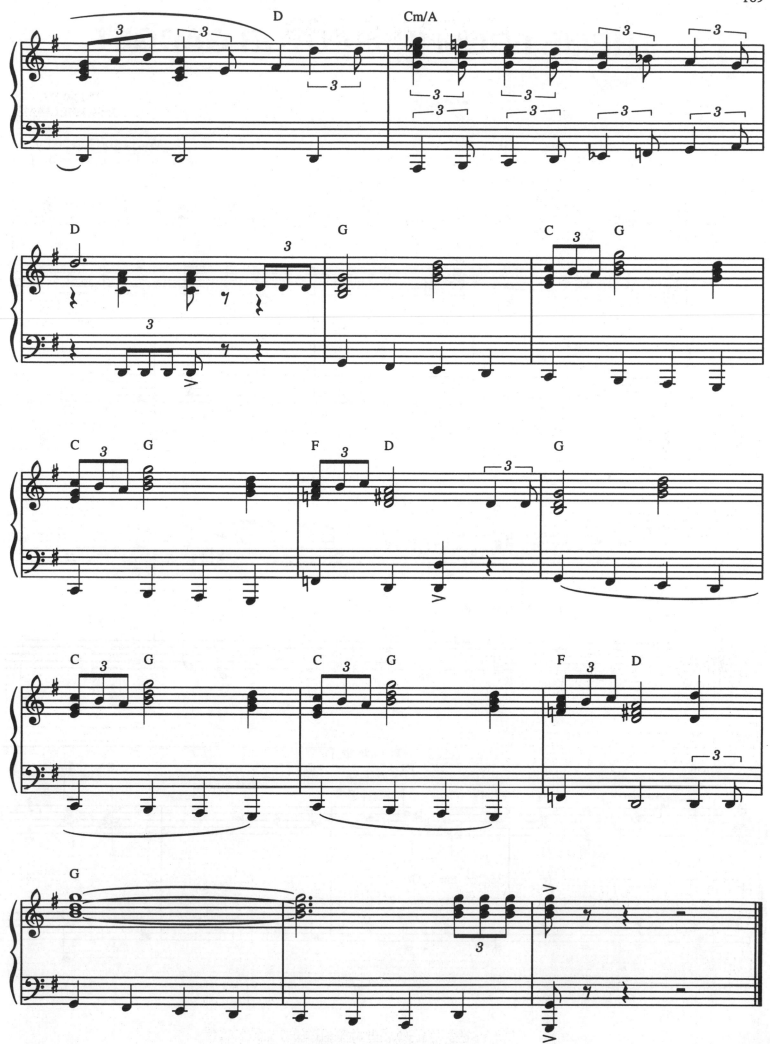

169

Star Wars - 2 - 2

THEME FROM INSPECTOR GADGET

Words and Music by
HAIM SABAN and SHUKI LEVY

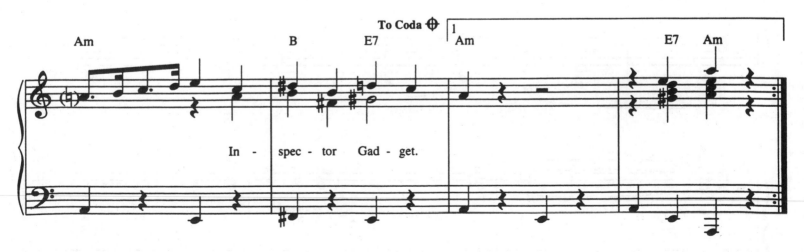

Theme From Inspector Gadget - 2 - 1

THEMES FROM "BATMAN FOREVER"
(Main Title/Rooftop Seduction Theme)

Composed by
ELLIOT GOLDENTHAL

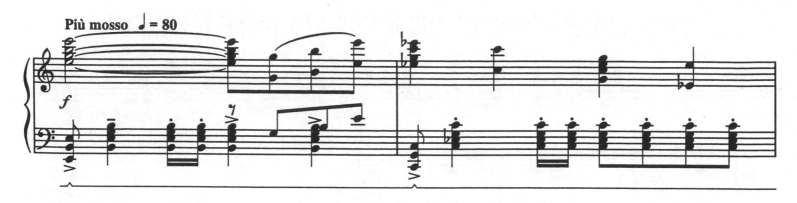

Themes From "Batman Forever" - 4 - 2

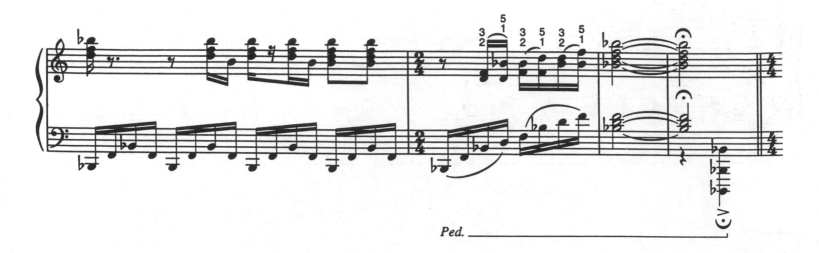

Rooftop Seduction Theme

Sultry & sensuous ♩ = 78

A tempo

WHO LET THE DOGS OUT

Words and Music by
ANSLEM DOUGLAS

Who Let the Dogs Out - 7 - 4

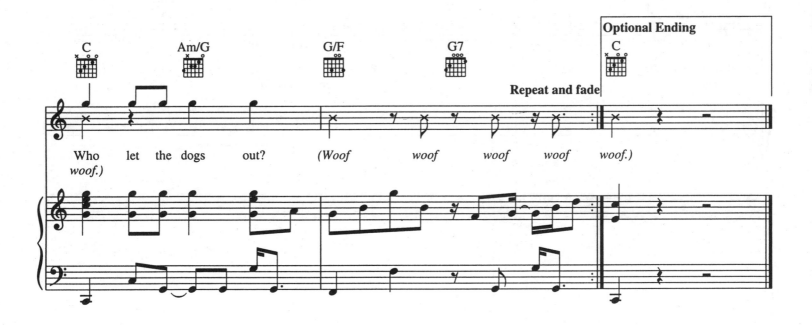

Additional Lyrics

Well if I am a dog, the party is on.
I gotta get my groove on 'cause my mind done gone.
Do you see the ray comin' from my eye,
Walkin' through the place like Digi-man
Just breakin' it down.
Me and my white silk shorts I can't see color.
Any color will do. I'll stick on you,
That's why they call me pit bull.
'Cause I'm a man of the land;
When they see me they say ooh.

THE WIND BENEATH MY WINGS

Words and Music by
LARRY HENLEY and JEFF SILBAR

The Wind Beneath My Wings - 7 - 1

The Wind Beneath My Wings - 7 - 7

From Warner Bros. Pictures' HARRY POTTER AND THE PRISONER OF AZKABAN

A WINDOW TO THE PAST

Music by
JOHN WILLIAMS

Slowly and tenderly (♩. = 54)

A Window to the Past - 3 - 1

Tempo I

ff

mp

8vb

p

dim. e rit.

pp